www.LonSafko.com

Copyright © 2016, Lon Safko.

ISBN-13: 978-1537657189

ISBN-10: 1537657186

All rights reserved. This book may not be reproduced, in whole or part, in any form without written permission of the copyright owner.

Created in the United States of America.

This is book was created using 100% recycled electrons.

No animals were harmed in the making of this book.

This book is dolphin safe.

www.LonSafko.com

www.LonSafko.com

Contents

Introduction.

Everybody Isn't Your Demographic

Mass Marketing - Is Expensive

Prospects Who Could Become Customers

The 1.54 Second & The 5 Second Rules

Advertising Conversion

Those Who Become Aware

Volume of Sales Leads

Awareness

Traditional, Email, Web, And Social Media

Conversion - Very Low

Conversion – Low

Conversion – Moderate

Conversion – High

Awareness - Marketing and Activity

Build Brand - Advertise, Email Blast, SEO & SEM & Social Participation

Search - Frame Buying Decision & Respond, Build Relationship

Research - Directly Complete & Follow Up, Build Trust, & Ecommerce

Purchase - Close & Sell

Awareness Cycle

Sales Cycle

Cost of Customer Acquisition

Repeat Customers

Summary: Three Ways to Increase Revenue

www.LonSafko.com

Introduction

I have been studying sales, marketing, and the "sales funnel" for more than 30 years. There have been many iterations of the funnel over the past three decades. This has made it easier for myself and many others in business. Helping us to understand the mind set and activities necessary to convert people to prospects then prospects to customers. The problem with the previous sales funnels were, they never really seem to tell the whole story. Many pieces of the prospects mindset were unaccounted for. Here is a new version of the age old sales funnel, The Ultimate Sales Funnel that finally tells the whole story.

Included is the visual graphic of the sales funnel that shows all of its intricate components. Take a moment to look at The Ultimate Sales Funnel image. It is the only image you are going to see throughout this book. It is all you need. Please refer back to this image as we discuss all of its components. You will recognize many of the pieces from previous funnel images, but maybe not all. Here is The Ultimate Sales Funnel.

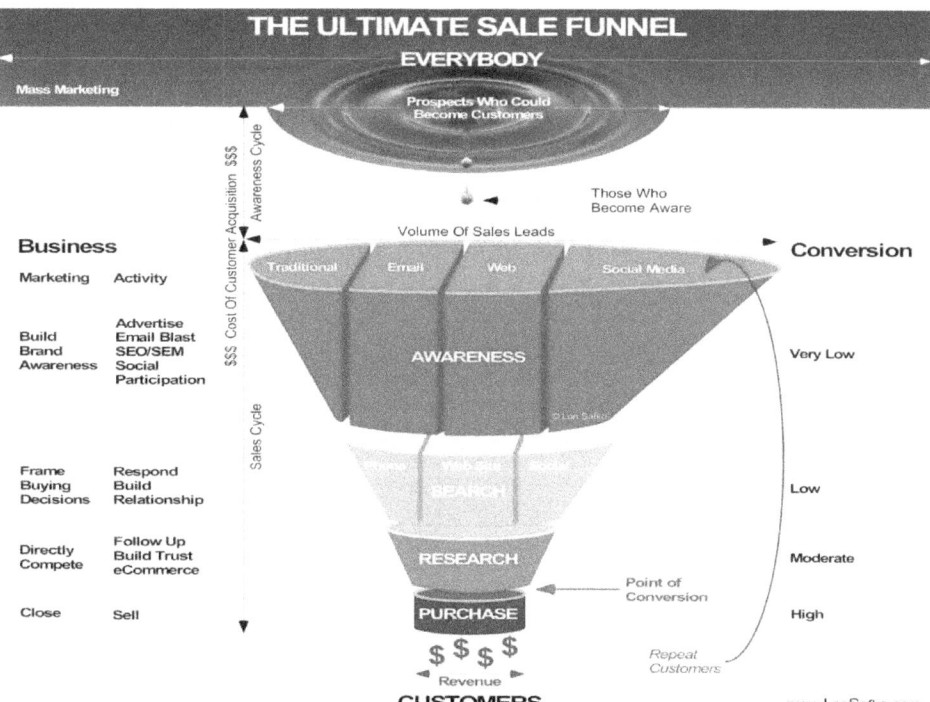

Please scan the image, or click the link below for a larger copy of the picture on the previous page.

http://lonsafko.com/Lon_Safko_The_Ultimate_Sales_Funnel.jpg

www.LonSafko.com

EVERYBODY - Isn't Your Demographic

Start at the top with the label "EVERYBODY". Everybody you are able to reach with your mass marketing message. Whether it was through a newspaper, magazine ads, your social media platforms, email blast, television or radio commercial, web site, or even a trade show. The first step in reaching "everybody" is through mass marketing. This is where you push a lot of information out to a lot of people through a multitude of different platforms, costing a great deal of money.

Mass advertising or mass marketing is ineffective and when using traditional marketing, often expensive. As marketers, we are willing to pay the high costs with extremely low conversion rates of mass marketing. We know that if we want to hit that 1 in a million person who might convert to a customer and generate revenue, we have to get our message in front of a million people. We also know that if we need 10 customers each day, then the math is simple, we need to get in front of 10 million new people every day to convert ten customers. Warning: Your math may vary.

Throughout this book, we will use a new car as the example "product" as seen from the eyes of the auto dealership as the "business". Please keep in mind, the new car is only an example for demonstration purposes. Any product or service or your product or service will work within this discussion.

Using the new car example, by advertising in the newspaper (53% of all new car advertising dollars are spent on newspaper advertising), you know that of the 1m, 500,000, 200,000 impressions newspapers offers, only an extremely small percent will convert. Out of an average 100 people off the streets, probably 0% will be interested in talking about buying a new car at that particular moment. The buying cycle for a new car is measured in years. More on the buying cycle later in this book. The chances of selecting even 1 out of that 100 people who at that exact moment are ready to buy a new car (or your product), is extreme.

Mass Marketing - Is Expensive

Mass marketing is something we all experience every day and have since we were born. A recent study showed we are exposed to between 5,000 and 10,000 advertisements, spam, unsolicited commercial messages every day. They come in the form of Television ads, radio commercials, newspaper and magazine ads, email blasts, banner ads, junk mail, billboards, and the list goes on.

Mass marketing is designed to build brand awareness. We will discuss awareness more as we proceed. When a prospect becomes "aware" they need a product or service like yours, you hope that it's your brand, company, logo, slogan, jingle, or product they think of first. If not, you risk them finding your competitors product before yours as they enter their search mode of their buying cycle. You have then lost that customer forever, or, at least for the next buying cycle.

Prospects Who Could Become Customers

Not everybody who sees your advertising message could become a customer. Some people will never buy your product or service no matter how many times you advertise to them, how many ads they see, whatever amount of discount your offer them. Only a small percentage of random people off the street would ever need your product and need it at that exact moment you decided to advertise.

Billions of dollars are spent each year on mass marketing to build brand recognition. Last night, what TV commercial did you see? Was it for a new car or truck? Was it for fast food? Was it for a new prescription medication? I'll bet you can remember the truck company or the fast food company. That's how it works. The advertisers are spending huge amounts of money hoping that today, when you think about lunch, you think "I'm' lovin' it!"

By creating dozens of impressions of that brand, your short term memory converts that image or sound into a long term memory, much the same way, practicing playing a piano or riding bike goes from short term to long term. This way, when you are actually ready to buy a product or service like the advertiser's, you think of them first.

By the way, did you run out last night after seeing the repetitive commercials, but a new truck? a hamburger? No... Because you weren't ready to buy. That's the problem with mass marketing. It has to be done a lot over a long period of time to have any effect on the decision making of your prospect.

This type of advertising is extremely expensive and most mid-sized and small companies cannot afford mass marketing advertising. We must be more selective and choose where and when we spend our precious advertising dollars. If our limited advertising isn't repetitive enough to drive our message into the long term memory of our prospect, it has to be memorable enough to get their attention and get them to react (convert). Our ad has to have something that catches our prospects eye, locks them in, engages them, and gets them to read or listen to our entire message. And, we have an incredibly short time to do that.

The 1.54 Second & The 5 Second Rules

In my bestselling books, The Social Media Bible and again in The Fusion Marketing Bible, I introduce the "1.54 Second & 5 Second Rules of Advertising conversion concept.

Several years ago, there was a study completed that tested how people react to advertising in magazines. They put dozens of subjects in a chair, gave them a magazine, and equipped them with special glasses that would track their eye movements as they read the magazine.

They quickly found as they turned a page, they started in the top left hand corner (an American and English language custom). Then began scanning from left to right continuing this way down the page. Once at the bottom of the page, the reader would begin again at the top left of the next page. Their eyes only stopped for two reasons, either there was an article they were interested in and they began to read the article or they saw an ad that got their attention.

As they studied the readers stopping for the ads, they found the reader stopped for only 1.54 seconds to determine whether or not the ad had information that interested them. In order to get the reader to stop for 1.54 seconds, the headline of that article really had to grab their attention. If the headline was provocative enough, the reader would then grant the ad 5 more seconds to determine whether the next text was also attention grabbing and relevant. If it was, the reader would read the entire ad. If that 5 seconds was not of interest, the reader would simply turn the page eliminating that advertiser forever.

After reading this study, I realized the 1.54 Second Rule meant there had to be a killer headline or image (a picture is worth a 1,000 words), or the reader (prospect) was lost forever. The 1.54 seconds was exactly the amount of time it takes to read a typical print ad headline, usually consisting of 5 words or less. Next, it had to be a well-crafted first sentence grabbing the reader's attention or again, they would turn the page and you, the advertiser would lose them forever. A typical sentence takes about 5 seconds to read and comprehend.

Thinking about how important the results of this magazine advertising study was, I knew there had to be other applications. It obviously also applies to newspapers, but what about other forms of advertising? What about television? Of course! The initial image or opening line has to capture your attention immediately otherwise you would change the channel, head off to the bathroom, or the kitchen. What about radio? Of course! The opening line has to stop you dead in your tracks so you will listen to the remaining 28 seconds of the commercial. We've all heard the announcer yelling "Sunday! Sunday! Sunday!", which usually gets our attention.

What about other forms of advertising, say digital? Yes! The image and headline on your web site will either get your visitor to stay and read on, click the back-button, close the page. This is call web page "stickiness".

What about email? Absolutely! What is your 1.54 second attention grabber? Your subject line! This is why your subject line is the most important part of email advertising. You know yourself... After maybe looking at the sender's name, you make a determination whether or not to open the email or hit the delete button based on the subject line. And, the time it takes to make that decision is 1.54 seconds.

Once your reader opens your email, the first sentence better be worth their time. Exactly 5 seconds of their time or it's the delete button again. Once the delete button has been hit, you have lost the prospect forever, or at least until the next email campaign.

The 1.54 Second and the 5 Second Rules apply to all forms of advertising whether it's traditional, digital, or social marketing. These are also the first two critical levels of conversion.

Advertising Conversion

All advertising has multiple levels of conversation. You need to stop thinking the only definition of conversation is the sale. The sale is important, but getting to it is even more important. If you do everything correctly, nothing goes wrong, then you successfully complete every level of conversion, the result is a sale. A sale is what happened if your do everything before it, correct.

As an example, newspaper advertising has many levels of conversion. The first level is actually getting the ad in the newspaper. You could be late with the ad, the newspaper might not place it on time, spelling or image issues can happen, or the ad could get pulled. Many things can go wrong preventing your "everybody" from seeing your ad. It's your job to have a plan for the process of getting your ad successfully placed in that newspaper on any given day.

This holds true for television, radio, pay-per-click advertising, banner ads, email blasts, etc. Work through every step and have a deliberate plan. You need a plan to get it to work in the first place and a plan to fix it if it doesn't. If it fails for any myriad of reasons, your "everybody", "prospect", and "customer" will never see your ad. That opportunity is lost forever (or at least until your next advertising expenditure cycle).

When your ad does make it into the newspaper successfully, the paper itself needs to have a plan to get it delivered. Once again, for every one of your "everyone" that doesn't get the newspaper, your opportunity is lost forever again. Next conversion is, the recipient needs to find the newspaper, pick it up, and actually read it. Often, it just moves from the driveway to the recycle bin. Your expensive opportunity is lost again.

Once the reader gets the paper, finds it, and makes the time to read it, it's really up to us to get our information through the remaining conversion levels. This is where the 1.54 Second & the 5 Second Rules come into play. There again, the headline or image and a first sentence has to immediately capture the reader's attention, or... They turn the page and move on. Whether it's turning the page, changing the channel, turning the dial, hitting delete, clicking the back-button, to selecting your competitors link, you lose. Your opportunity lost forever.

Those Who Become Aware

Those who become aware are those everybody's that have passed the test of seeing your advertising, which is a difficult and expensive process for the advertiser, then deciding they could become a customer someday. As a small percentage filters through the mass marketing, it drips into your sales funnel. This drip might come in from traditional marketing, email marketing, web sites, SEO (Search Engine Optimization), SEM (Search Engine Marketing or Pay-Per-Click advertising), or through your social platforms such as Facebook, Twitter, Pinterest, Instagram, LinkedIn, or another platform.

As the everybody filters through and drips into one of your funnel segments, they have moved from being an everybody into a becoming prospect. At this point, you now have a chance to convert them from being a prospect into a customer. It's our job the help them throughout the process of the sales cycle, moving them through the funnel to becoming a customer.

It's also our responsibility to keep mining the everybody's for more potential prospects starting by making them aware they need your product or service. Making them aware, you must then make them either react or remember your product or service until they start their buying cycle. It is every marketer's dream that once an everybody becomes aware, they immediately enter the funnel and begin their sales cycle.

Volume of Sales Leads

The volume of sales leads refers to the size of your funnel. How wide is your funnel? How many compartments does it have? How big is each compartment? It's easy to figure out. How many newspapers are you advertising in and what are their impression rates. Impression rates are a non-sensical number to determine the actual readership of any periodical; however, it's the only thing we have unless you are measuring your conversions.

Add up the impressions from all of your traditional advertising, Facebook, Twitter, email lists, and your other advertising. At this point, you should have a pretty good idea how wide your funnel is. If you're not getting enough customers out of the bottom of your funnel the solution is simple, add more prospects to the top of the funnel. Add more traditional advertising, increase your email lists, increase you pay per-click budget, and increase your followers on your social networks.

Awareness

As I mentioned above, one of the first critical steps is to make your prospect "aware" of you, your product, and most importantly that they need your product. From here on out, I am going to refer to "product or service" as simply product.

Using the example of the new car, awareness means "I have thought about getting a new car… My car is getting kind of old… I do like the new model cars… I probably could afford taking on a reasonable car loan… I bet I could get a good trade in for my old car… Etc."

There is a process of bringing your everybody to this mindset before they start into the sales funnel. As you are designing your mass market advertising, try to keep in mind you are not necessarily closing the sale. The mindset of someone who hadn't thought about purchasing a product like yours needs to be changed into a state where they become aware and start thinking "What if I buy?", which begins the process.

Traditional, Email, Web, And Social Media

Traditional

We use these primary categories for mass market advertising. Traditional marketing such as newspaper, magazine, television, radio, etc. is a good way to get your message in front of a lot of everybody's, if you can afford it. That is the problem today with traditional marketing. It's expensive and less and less people are participating.

Email

Email is my favorite form of mass marketing. My lists are double opted-in, meaning they asked to be put on my lists then they are asked to confirmed they want to be on my lists. I also make it easy for them to unsubscribe. Following all of the rules of the 2004 Can Spam Act and the 2014 Canada Anti-Spam Law (CASL). Remember, anyone who doesn't have a relationship with you, won't buy from you. When you have a strong large list with people who know who you are, they will convert. They will buy.

Web

For two decades the web has been around and now has finally matured. Nearly everyone on earth has access to the Internet and it is up to us as marketers to take advantage of that opportunity. We need to make digital marketing tools part of every marketing plan we build.

The difference between traditional marketing, digital marketing and social media marketing is this. Traditional marketing has been done the same way for 6,000 years. Traditional marketing is considered "push" marketing. We push our message out to the masses and wait to see if we sell. It's a monologue. There isn't a two-way communication. This hasn't changed in six millenniums. We place an ad and hope for the best.

Social Media Marketing implies that there is a two-way conversation, a dialogue. When we post a blog, we expect to see comments. When we tweet, we expect to see retweets. When we "pin" something on Pinterest, we expect to see it re-pinned. We expect that response, a dialogue.

I've always considered email marketing to be the original social media marketing. It's using a digital network just like social media and it implies a two-way conversation. Everything we start on social media, usually closes on email.

Digital Marketing is technology based, but doesn't imply a conversation. Tools such as SEO (Search Engine Optimization), SEM (Search Engine Marketing or Pay-Per Click), e-commerce, and RSS (Really Simple Syndication) where you place a button on your blog site where allows your visitor to sign up, then they will automatically get a notice whenever you update your blog. This doesn't include a conversation.

The web is an amazing way to toss a really large net and allow a huge amount of everybody's to hear your marketing message. And, for the most part, it's relatively easy and inexpensive to do. RSS is a onetime code add to your blog site. SEO is a one time (every couple of years), tweaking of your web page code. Email marketing is almost always free or nearly free. The only category where it is intended for you to spend money, is SEM or PPC, and the amount you spend each month is up to you.

Conversion - Very Low

Unfortunately, the awareness segment of your sales funnel has the lowest conversion rate. When your prospects enter at this level, they are newly aware they may need your product. They haven't thought about it enough to make a decision about the type of product, who they will eventually purchase it from, or what they are willing to pay for it.

To use our new car example, at this stage the prospect only now admits that they might need to consider buying a new car. They don't know what make, model, color, size, or price. They only know they should think about it more.

Remember, when advertising to prospects in this category, you can use general high-level keywords. These keywords are less expensive and will convert better than ones that are very specific. Advertise to the mindset of the prospect to capture them at the level of where they are in the sales cycle.

When our prospects are in this segment, it is our opportunity as marketers to nurture these leads, build a relationship with them, and guide them through the next segment of the funnel, search.

Search

When our prospects enter this segment of the sales funnel, they are more committed to the idea of purchasing yours (or competitors) product. By now they have made to decision to purchase only. They still don't have any details. This is where they begin their search for products, prices, and people to buy it from.

Phone, Web Site, Social

Today, most people start their searches on the web, making your web site or e-commerce site very handy. And your SEO! If they can't find you, to them, you don't exist. If they do find your competitor, most likely, won't have them as a customer.

If you are active on social platforms, and I strongly recommend you are, the second place people search for product and reviews are on social media. While your web site is critical, it is irrelevant. When prospects are in the search mode, they need to find your web site easily or you lose. It builds credibility in the product and in your organization. Once they find it, they generally don't care at all about what you have to say about yourself.

We've abused our web sites by saying "We are the world leader in providing world class leadership in leading the world thought leadership and worldly leaders…" or whatever our lousy mission statements say. They're all at the same and useless. When was the last time you read all of the text on a home page? I rest my case.

You have to be there to be in the game, but once they confirm you're real, it back to Facebook to find a half dozen people who have had personal experiences with you and your product. Peer review is more important to a prospect than anything you have to say about yourself.

If you have a brick & mortar location(s), then you might field telephone calls and walk-ins requisition information. Be prepared to provide that particular type of answers. Telling a prospect how much a car costs at this stage of the sales cycle would be counterproductive and would not close the sale. It might actually push the prospect to your competitor. It's too soon for that information.

Conversion – Low

At this segment of the sales cycle, the conversion rate will be very low. The prospect is still at the search, high level of their thought process. Again, it's our responsibility as a marketer to lead the prospect through the sales cycle and down into the next level of research. Keep in mind, we have to allow our prospects to move at their own pace through the process. Forcing them to move faster will make them uncomfortable and could scare them away.

Research

The research segment of the sales funnel is critical. This is the final step of information gathering before they convert, purchase. At this point in the cycle, your prospect is asking more specific questions. Now it's about warranty, color, make, model, and price. This is where they are making their final decisions on exactly what product they will buy and from whom they will but it. At this point, you need to have built a relationship of trust with your prospect. A good relationship will often overcome price concerns. How many times in the past have you paid more for a product just because you like the seller? Have you ever bought anything at Nordstrom's? Likely, you could have gotten the product cheaper on line, but you still were willing to pay more because of your brand relationship with Nordstrom's.

Think of other times you were willing to pay more. Build a relationship like that with your prospects and they will buy from you.

Conversion – Moderate

The final decisions are made at this time, especially about you and your competitors. The conversation during this process is good, moderate. At the end of this segment of the cycle the conversion happens. Up until then, you could still loose the prospect to either your competitor or to a no sale.

Remember: Use very specific keywords to attract prospects in the research mode. They are ready to make their final decision here. For example, have a web page or Facebook page that specifically talks about the final decision making information; make model, color, warranty, and price. Now is the time to position your project for the close. Make it easy for them to find the specific information they need to make a buying decision.

Purchase

Here we are, at the moment of truth. If you've done everything correct up until now, they will convert. They will convert from a prospect to a customer then you will reap the rewards of revenue. Now you can see why, earlier, I stressed the concept of conversion. Conversion is not the sale. It's all of the steps we discussed until now, which will make or break the sale. If our prospect doesn't convert at every step of the way, we lose them.

We need to think through each of the steps to make sure we have them all covered. We need to make sure our prospect gets the specific level of information they require. We have to provide them with that information, not something different. As I said earlier, if we do everything right up until this point... The final conversion or the sale will happen.

Conversion – High

Of course the conversion rate is high at this point. The prospect has gathered all of the information they need to make their buying decision. This is where they convert to paying customers, and all the hard work and preparation come to fruition.

Business

This side of the Ultimate Sales Funnel image is the business side. As your prospect moves their way through the funnel, as the business, you must react to their mind set, helping them through the funnel to conversation. Each step of their journey requires you to respond differently. Above, you have read the keywords to use in Pay-Per Click and SEO changes as your prospects moves through the different stages of buying. You need to be aware and nurture those prospect to keep them in the funnel and ultimately, convert them to customers.

Awareness - Marketing and Activity

Build Brand - Advertise, Email Blast, SEO & SEM and Social Participation

This is the early stage where your prospect has just become aware of their problem or desire. The types of questions they are asking are very high level, general, and vague. This is where mass marketing using traditional media, building and communicating with your email list, and having your SEO, SEM, RSS in place. Also having a strong presence on all the most popular social media platforms is important. In this stage, it is all about getting your brand out there so it can be seen by the uneducated prospect.

Search - Frame Buying Decision & Respond, Build Relationship

During this stage of the sales cycle, it's very important as the nurturing company, to frame the buying decision for your prospect. Here, you attempt to connect with your prospect on a one-on-one basis. Be available to answer questions by phone. Have a FAQ (Frequently Asked Questions Page easy to find on the web. Monitor all of your social networks closely and in a timely manner, so there is a quick response to any questions needing to be addressed.

The goal of this segment is to build a relationship with your prospect. You, as a company need to build their confidence so you can provide the right solution for their problem. You need to be there for your prospect with information, conversations, and reasons to buy.

Research - Directly Complete and Follow Up, Build Trust, And e-commerce

Marketing Leads to Relationships, Relationships Lead to Trust, Trust Sells

The research segment is the last chance you will have before your prospect begins to finalize their buying decision. During this stage, you must be very responsive to their queries. 24 hours is often too long to wait for a response. Set Google Alerts to monitor Internet conversation and respond immediately.

During this stage, your primary goal is to build trust. Trust sells. You generally wouldn't buy something (especially a large ticketed item) from someone you didn't trust. Relationships leads to trust. Trust leads to revenue.

Purchase - Close and Sell

Finally, your prospect has gone through his buying journey, asked all the questions, chosen the right make, model, and price for them. Then, most importantly, chose you to buy from. It's now your job to close the sale and convert the prospect from a prospect into a customer. The sale is yours to lose or yours to win.

You need to ask a lot of insightful questions about yourself, your organization, your staff, and your technology. Is your staff properly trained and friendly? Are they dressed appropriately. Does your brick-and-mortar location look it's best? Does it build trust? Does it make the prospect confident they have made the right choice?

Does your e-commerce site look good? Does it navigate well? Have you tried your shopping cart lately? How does it work? Is it intuitive? Will it make your prospect close out of it and go to the competitor?

Are other customers saying good things about you and your product on the social media platforms? Have you posted dozens of videos of happy customers on YouTube? When you prospect sees other happy customers, they project themselves as happy customers. Respond to their posts, tweets, and updates as soon as possible. Possibly, it will be the moment they decide to buy?

If you said yes to all of the above, then you most likely will have passed all of the conversion check points. Most likely, your prospects would not have found reasons to leave the funnel. And, as I discussed above, if you have done everything right, the final conversion is the sale, revenue, success.

Awareness Cycle

To summarize this label, the Awareness Cycle is the amount of time and marketing necessary to take the brand new prospect from their first realization to a point where they decide to start the buying process. This is often an expansive and time consuming cycle. It requires a lot of advertising and time for the initial prospect to decide to begin the sales process. There are no guarantees the new prospect will continue on their buying journey. The dropout rate is very high here. Often the prospect will leave, sometimes forever; however, sometimes they will return, even multiple times.

Sales Cycle

We discussed the sales cycle a great deal throughout this book and I hope you have a good understanding of what it is and how it effects the sales process. What most marketers don't realize is, that every product we purchase from a pack of breath mints to a new Mercedes follows the exact same thinking process. The only difference is, the larger the price, the longer the sales cycle. And the reverse is also true, the less expensive the purchase, the faster we all move through the sales cycle.

The example I used throughout the book was a new car. When was the last time you bought a new car; three years ago, four, five, more? From the time you realized or became aware you wanted (needed) a new car did you drive that car off the lot? Another 6 months? A year? More? A new car is an expensive purchase and its corresponding sales cycle is long.

A box of breath mints works the same way. You are in the checkout line waiting for the person ahead of you to check out. Your eyes are scanning the "impulse" items (that's what all the little trinkets, candies, gums, newspapers, and horoscope booklets are called surrounding the both side of the checkout isle.)

As you scan the items, you first become aware. You say to yourself "I think I need some breath mints." Then you look around and find the rack with all of the manufacturers many different flavors, shapes, and packages.

Then your search. You say to yourself "I like Tic-Tacs!" So, you search for the section of the rack that holds Tic-Tacs.

Next, you research. You say to yourself "I like the Fresh Mint better than the Passion Fruit mints." So, you research that small segment of the Tic-Tac rack until you find the Fresh Mint Tic-Tacs, and bam… You grab a box and throw them on the conveyor belt. You converted to a purchase.

Instead of this process taking 3, 4 or 5 year as it did with the new car, the exact same process unfolded in under 30 seconds. Remember how we all start with awareness then end up at the purchase. Only the cycle length changes, which will help you market more effectively.

Cost of Customer Acquisition

The Cost of Customer Acquisition is in my opinion, one of the most important metrics you have. How else can you measure or determine how good a job you are doing? If you're not completely familiar with the definition, it's the cost your company incurs creating one customer.

The easiest way to calculate this number, is to take how much your company spent last year and how many new customers did you have. Then, divide the costs by the number of customers. I think if you take the time to calculate this number, you will be shocked by how high your costs are for each and every new customer.

You can fine tune this number by subtracting out repeat customers and other itemized costs that were spent, not generating new customers. Please remember, your costs were not just advertising costs. To generate customers, you need a lot of support. Could new customers be generated without your payroll expense? The payroll of all who helped with the advertising, finance, web design, business cards, postage, even the building that you work in? Did you develop your advertising from a park bench? Probably not.

Sophisticated, Fortune 500 know their cost of customer acquisition very well. While these number are very difficult to find, here are some estimates of cost of customer acquisition for companies and industries you are familiar with.

Travel	
priceline.com	$7

Retail	
Index of 74 Retailers:	$14
Barnes & Noble:	$10
Amazon:	$29

Magazines	
Consumer Magazines:	$48

Satellite / Cable

XM Sirius:	$123
Cable Companies:	$150
Direct Satellite:	$400
Direct TV:	$550

Telecom

Sprint:	$315

Financial

Credit Cards	$150
TD Waterhouse:	$175
Ameritrade:	$202
E-Trade:	$272
Mortgages:	$300-$700

Vehicles

Recreation Vehicles:	$900

Homes

New Homes:	$2,100

As you can see, the cost of generating one single customer is huge for most companies and probably is very high for your company (But, you won't know until you do the math...)

Now you understand when a customer tries to cancel a credit card, the customer service rep works you so hard. They are willing to forgive fees, lower interest rates, anything to get you to stay. The math for them is simple. If it costs them $150 to replace you as a customer, they can give away up to $150 in fees and rates to keep you and still make money. It's cheaper to keep you than it is to replace you.

That is also why it costs $180 to cancel a cell phone contract. They want you to pay them their cost of customer acquisition if they have to replace you!

Repeat Customers

This leads us to repeat customers. Way too often we forget about our existing customers. It is far easier and much cheaper to push that old customer back to the top of the sales funnel and out the revenue end than it is to start over with a new prospect. The existing customer already had their questions answered. You have already built a relationship with them. That relationship lead to trust and ultimately a sale.

The next time you sit down to develop your next marketing plan, take some time to consider developing a plan just for turning existing customers into repeat customers. This is the most profitable customer of all.

A repeat customer is less expensive to sell to, the cost of customer acquisition is much less because they bypass your marketing, they move more quickly through the funnel, and have a significantly higher conversion rate.

Summary: Three Ways to Increase Revenue

If you want to increase revenue, there are only three variables you need to consider; the width of the top funnel, the height of the funnel, and the width of the bottom of the funnel. In other words; The number of sales leads entering the funnel, the length of the sales cycle, and the effectiveness of your conversation. Making the funnel wider at the top or increasing the number of qualified leads will increase revenue. Shortening the height of the funnel or reducing the sales cycle will increase revenue, or widening the exit of the funnel or increasing your conversion rate will increase revenue.

Any one of these can increase revenue and by improving two or all three functions will dramatically increase your revenue. The one remaining factor that can increase revenue is deliberately developing a system or program to push your recent customers, back into the funnel from the top.

To many businesses forget to use this additional step and miss out on easy, faster revenue. A happy existing customer is already aware of your business and your offering, so the awareness cycles is eliminated. And as they are already aware, your mass market costs are eliminated. The existing customer has already gone through the sales cycle with your business and pass through the funnel at a quicker rate.

I hope this diagram and discussion has helped you to better understand the mind set of your customer. The process a prospect goes through from the first time they hear about you and your product through their purchase. Creating this diagram really help me to see the entire process in one image.

If you like this book, please give it a review on Amazon. For more information on me, visit www.LonSafko.com or connect with me on Facebook or LinkedIn!

Lon Safko

www.LonSafko.com